Moolah

7 Principles of Getting Out of Debt

Brandie Hill

Dedication

To all those individuals who made poor financial decisions and want a second chance to live life abundantly.

Acknowledgements

I realize we don't walk this life alone. First, I thank God for His inspiration and everlasting love. Secondly, I would like to thank my past for teaching me these valuable lessons. Without my past, I would not be able to share this book with you and I would not know the excitement of being on the brink of destiny.

I thank my brothers, Jeff and Lloyd, for always pushing and supporting me. I thank my parents for continuing to smile upon me although they are no longer on this earth and I thank them for teaching me to persevere through all. I especially thank my mom for her enduring strength. I thank my spiritual sisters (Stephanie, Valarie, Charlotte, Rachel, Cassandra, Krystal, and Jennifer) for being my undying support team and a dynamic group of women. Because of you I am a better woman. I thank my pastor, Bishop Brandon B. Porter, for his teaching, encouragement, and love.

I would like to thank Tammie Taylor for inspiring me to write a book and for sharing her knowledge. I pray that you are richly blessed.

Last, but not least, to the host of friends, family, and loved ones whose names I didn't have room to include, I thank you for just being you. Your love, support, encouragement, and words of life are priceless. You have encouraged me in times you were unaware.

Contents

Preface:

Have you ever felt like you should be in a better place financially? Have you ever looked back over the years and analyzed all the bad financial decisions you've made and literally cried? Well, if you answered yes to either or both of these questions, we're in the same boat because I have too!

For many years, I longed to be in a better financial position. I agonized over the amount of money I was making but unable to enjoy much of because of poor, past decisions. Bill after bill had to be paid, food had to be put on the table, and by the time I got to the end of the to-do list, the money left for me was skim. And then, the recession hit. Now it seemed money was even tighter, companies were laying off, reducing income, minimizing 401k plans, and taking away bonuses. My plan for a better life seemed to be pushed further out. If one was to look at the situation, they would think there was no hope. But, I soon realized this was the perfect storm for opportunity. That's right, an opportunity to get my financial freedom and life back on track. During this time, I learned 7 key principles that have lead me to financial stability and the expectation of a better life. I've decided to share these principles with you to help you get out of the rut you are in and to encourage you to know that there is hope for your financial dilemma.

So, let's get started! If you apply these basic principles to your life and decision making, I believe you will be happier and just as excited as I am for what lies ahead……..FREEDOM!

Principle 1: The Law of Sowing and Reaping

The law of sowing and reaping is a law most people don't want to think or talk about, but it's very essential to your financial prosperity. No matter what your religious belief is or lack thereof, there is a common law at work. Just like the law of gravity, the law of sowing and reaping is at work whether you want to believe it or not.

As a Christian, I am a firm believer in *Galatians 6:7 Be not deceived; God is not mocked: for whatsoever a man **soweth**, that shall he also reap.*

Now this particular scripture is referring to anything that is sown: money, love, hate, food, etc. If you sow money, you shall reap money. If you sow love, you shall reap love and so forth.

Oftentimes, we want to reap things for which we have not sown. Understanding this principle is essential for your debt deliverance. To get out of debt, you need money and favor. Therefore you need to sow money and favor. Let's look at a practical example, farmers. I have never had to work on a farm, but from what I've been told, farming is not easy. You have to till the soil, work the soil, plant the seed, water the seed, and then harvest the seed. What farmer do you know who plants corn and does all the work to harvest corn, and then expects tomatoes??? The answer is none, because the farmer understands the law of sowing and reaping.....you harvest what you plant. The same law is at work in every aspect of our lives. If you expect to receive money you have to plant and release money.

Now, you may not be a Christian and believe this law is erroneous but, I would pose to you that even non-Christians understand this basic law. Some say it as an old proverb, you reap what you sow and other faiths refer to it as Karma. The point is nature shows us this law is at work.

For me, understanding and believing this principle was the foundation for my getting back on track financially. Even when times were rough and I was down to my very last, trying to figure out what I was going to eat or how I would make it one more day, I had to trust and sow my tithe and offering. Why? Because I am convinced that this is something I can not afford not to do; I have to keep sowing.

Malachi 3:10 *says- Bring ye all the tithes into the storehouse, that there may be meat in mine house, and prove me now herewith, saith the LORD of hosts, if I will not open you the windows of heaven, and pour you out a blessing, that there shall not be room enough to receive it.*

God has always proven Himself to me. Let me share with you one incident: for about four months straight, it appeared that I was getting back on track. Each month I would look at my budget and get excited because I expected to save a little more money. Each time though, something else would rear its head that would take all the excitement away: the garage door broke and had to be fixed; the creditor who would no longer accept a smaller monthly payment required a lump sum to avoid legal action so had to be paid; roof damage due to bad weather and had to be repaired; the list goes on and on. I was very discouraged, but I continued to pay my tithe and give offerings, not just because of my love for God, but because of my understanding of Principle 1: The Law of Sowing and Reaping. I had resolved in my mind in November that I wasn't going to allow this financial hell to affect my joy. Well, towards the end of November, our Pastor's Appreciation was near and I was contemplating how I would sow this seed because I really did not have it nor anything close to the amount the committee was asking for. All of a sudden and out of nowhere, someone was interested in buying a car that had been sitting for three years and I had been trying and wanting to sell. I was so excited because I thought of all the things I could do financially, including sowing my Pastor's Appreciation seed. I said to myself, "God, if I can sell this car, I will sow my Pastor's Appreciation seed". The next day, I sold the car for more than what I was expecting and immediately sowed my gift for Pastor's Appreciation. As soon as I sowed what the committee asked each member to give, I received that seed right back. Now, that's the law of sowing and reaping at work! It doesn't always work that fast, but the law works. Just as some seeds take longer to germinate, the same applies to this law. But, if you are patient and believe, you will reap exactly what you have sown.

Principle 1: The Law of Sowing and Reaping is your foundation to financial freedom, but it's up to you to apply it. You have made bad decisions in the past, why not try it? If you are as bad as I was, then trying it couldn't make the situation any worse.

Principle 1 Work Lessons:

Question 1: Look around you and try to identify the law of sowing and reaping?

_____

_____

_____

_____

Question 2: Can you think of experiences in your life that could have been a result of the law of sowing and reaping?

_____

_____

_____

_____

Question 3: Moving forward, how will you apply this law to get out of debt?

_____

_____

_____

_____

Principle 1 Notes:

_____

_____

_____

_____

_____

_____

_____

_____

_____

_____

_____

_____

_____

_____

Principle 1 Thought Provoking Question:

What would happen if I forgave a debt someone owed me?

Reflection:

Principle 2: Learn to Live on Less to Live on More

The recession has really taught me how to live on less. I gave up things that I never thought I could live without. Many times, we have unnecessary bills because we want the latest and greatest. But if you really don't have the latest and greatest money to afford these items, you are doing more damage to yourself than living without them. I would venture to say that many times we only have some of these items because we are trying to keep up with our friends, neighbors, church members, co-workers or [in other words] *The Joneses.* There were items I had to eliminate. I had to be creative with food for breakfast, lunch, and dinner, and spend less on entertainment and fun. We will take a look at all of these items.

Unnecessary Technology

Let's examine some of the possible vices you may have:

Cell/Smart Phones

At the rapid pace at which technology is being developed, you could get a new phone every week and still someone else would have a newer or later model than yours. Ask yourself, do I really need this? How will I benefit from having this latest model? I guarantee you the manufacturer is the one who is benefiting. Have you examined your rate plan lately? Are you really taking advantage of the plan you have or are you just wasting money that could be applied elsewhere?

Wireless at home/ on the go

When did we become so disconnected? Ask yourself how many times you've used your wireless access at home away from your desk? Is this really a necessary expense you have to incur? I'm not one to discourage the use of technology, but when you are trying to eliminate debt, getting back to the basics is essential. With hotspots going up everywhere (hotels and restaurants, even McDonalds) offering free Wi-Fi, why incur an expense that someone else is willing to foot the bill for?

TV with over 300 channels

I have to admit, I am a bit of a TV junky and when I was forced to give up my satellite TV due to bad customer service, I was a little hurt at first. But, that didn't last vey long when I began saving $75 a month. I quickly learned to enjoy the programming on all the free channels! I warn individuals that are visiting my house, "you can watch TV on channels 3, 5, 13, 24, and 30" and they laugh. But I have come to enjoy the extra money I'm saving and the shows on those channels. Oftentimes, you may be asked if you saw this special or did you watch this show. You have to respond loudly 'NO, I don't have cable' to

convince yourself at first, but after a couple months it will no longer matter. Besides, how many times do you watch all 300 channels and now, you can practically watch every TV show on the internet anyway. Why pay for cable if you are already paying for internet access?

Learn to eliminate bills that cause what I call, double-dipping.

The **House Phone** is another bill that causes double-dipping. House phones are as extinct as dinosaurs so there's no longer a need for one. Ask yourself, why do you have a cell phone, house phone, and internet service? Now count up all the money you could be saving if you eliminated some of these. Many people try to use the excuse that they keep the house phone because of security alarms. Now-a-days even security monitoring companies offer plans connected to your cell phone. Also, if you have internet service, you can find voice-over IP carriers that allow you to make free phone calls from your computer. This is one bill I eliminated quickly.

Now, we have only examined four possible vices you may have, but there are a host of things that you could probably get rid of. Take a minute to list all of the items you are currently paying in one column. Out of that list, write down all the items you can eliminate in another column.

Current Bills	Bills I Can Eliminate

Creative Cooking

Food is an absolutely essential expense to incur. However, you can learn to appreciate other foods when you have to be creative, with less money. I will say that many of us know how to do this well and our ancestors taught us how to make food stretch. The only problem is many of our ancestors ate unhealthy foods that resulted in health problems. Unhealthy eating will only increase your medical bills later. So let's not swap one bill with another; but instead come up with ways to eat healthy and decrease our grocery bill each month.

For me, this 'sacrifice' was a little easier because I'm only cooking for one so whatever I cook, I'm satisfied with. However, if you have a family to feed, you may have to strike a balance to keep everyone happy. You could though take the stance of older generations and say 'you will eat whatever I put on the table and clean your plate'!

In this subset of the principle, I do have to give some credit to Dr. Ian Smith and his 50 Million Pound Challenge. I was trying to lose some weight and decided to take the challenge so I was following the steps and monitoring what I could and could not eat. In the first phase, you are restricted to certain foods. One of those foods is brown rice and I must say I have developed an affinity for it; it is now a staple of mine. So thank you Dr. Ian Smith. My grocery bill is less and I look better than I already did [I digressed but I'll get back to helping you get on track]!

Often times when trying to eat healthy, it seems as though your grocery bill is higher because of the fresh produce, leaner cuts of meat, and healthier desserts, if there is such a thing. But, I have found some items that are good for you and do not break your piggy back:

Cabbage

Brown Rice

Squash

Zucchini

Greens

Spinach

Broccoli

Eggs

Oatmeal

Green/Yellow/Red Peppers

Kidney Beans

The trick to lowering your grocery bill with these healthy items is to watch your weekly grocery circular. Many times you can get a lot of the vegetables mentioned above in the freezer section on sale: 10 for $10. Now that's a bargain!

There are quite a few recipes you can whip up with these healthy items. I know you may be skeptical so I will share one of my favorite recipes with you. I promise you will learn to love cooking creatively and if not, just picture dancing dollar signs in your head because that's what you'll be saving.

Before I share my recipe, I will give you a one day sample meal plan and some grocery shopping tricks. I was able to reduce my grocery bill from approximately $220 to $120 per month by following these tricks and sticking to these items.

One Day Meal Sample

Breakfast: Oatmeal

Lunch: Peanut Butter and Jelly Sandwich and an Apple

Dinner: Sautéed Vegetables over Brown Rice

Note: A full week meal plan can be found in the appendix.

Simple Tricks

- Stay on the outside lanes of the grocery store - healthier foods are always on the outside.

- Stock up on items when they are on sale, especially the frozen vegetables - you can always make a meal out of vegetables and rice.

- Clip coupons - any amount of savings is good savings.

- Purchase one indulgence - If you love ice cream, buy the one on sale that month or week. If you indulge in one of your loves or cravings every now and then, you won't be tempted to splurge.

My Special Recipe: Joy's Delight

Items you'll need:

1 can of organic Kidney Beans

1 fresh Squash

1 Fresh Zucchini

1 bag of Frozen 3 pepper blend (green/yellow/red peppers and onions)

1 Tomato

Extra Virgin Olive Oil

Brown Rice

Additional Items if you want to add meat

Deveined Shrimp

Jamaican Jerk Sauce

Directions:

Place a skillet on medium heat and cover bottom of pan with extra virgin olive oil. Wash the squash and zucchini, cut in medium pieces and place in skillet, sautéing 3-5 minutes. Place ¾ of the frozen pepper blend in the skillet and add ¼ cup of water. Simmer 10 minutes while watching the pan to avoid burning the squash and zucchini. Wash the tomato, cut in cubes and add to skillet. Add the organic kidney beans as well. Allow to cook for another 7 minutes. Stir the mix. Place on low and simmer.

In another pot bring water to a boil. Place 1 packet of brown rice and cook as directed.

Assembly for 1 serving:

Take half of the brown rice packet and place on plate. Take vegetables from skillet and place on top of brown rice.

Additional directions when adding meat

Take another skillet and cover bottom of skillet with extra virgin olive oil. Sauté shrimp. Take 2/3 Jamaican jerk sauce and add to skillet. Marinate shrimp in sauce for approximately 2 minutes. Remove shrimp from skillet and pour on top of already assembled plate.

And there you have a good meal!

Creative cooking can be fun and you will learn your taste buds actually enjoy other foods besides those you have been feeding them.

It's easy to find recipes online that incorporate these low cost items as well. It just takes a little planning, but you will reap the benefits by not spending so much each month on groceries.

Entertainment for Less

It's always hard to strike a balance with entertainment and fun and it's always hard to completely remove this from ones budget especially if you work hard. So, let's just do it cheaper.

Depending on what your taste is will determine how creative you have to be. But, I am a big movie junkie. So this was an easy fix for me. Instead of going out to the movies in which you can end up paying almost $20 for 1 movie and snacks, I subscribed to Netflix. It was the perfect relationship for me. Get as many movies as I wanted, send them back when I want to, and do it for the same price 1 movie would cost. It was a no brainer. Another great alternative these days for movie junkies is the Red Box. You only have to pay $1, you watch the movie that night, and then take it back. You can't beat $1 for a good movie.

If you are also a travel junkie like me, you can find great travel deals as well. The key is to travel in groups. If you can get a group of friends to go out of town and share in the expenses you can literally get out of town for a weekend for less than $70. The frequency of doing this depends on how deep in debt you are. If you can almost see the light at the end of the tunnel, a trip every now and then won't hurt your progress too much.

Living on Less to Live on More

Learning to live on less is definitely a process, but the process will reveal the unnecessary things you have depended on for so long. It will also unleash your creativity like never before. You might also find out things about yourself that you just didn't know. Most importantly, it will help you to free up cash to make a dent in your debt. The ultimate goal is to eliminate your debt and to become a better manager over your finances. Better decision making today by living on less will eventually allow you to live on more. Once you have learned to live on less or [a better way to put it] once you have been a good steward over little, He will make you ruler over much.

Principle 2 Work Lessons:

Action 1: List the unnecessary technology bills you plan to get rid of and by what date?

_____

_____

_____

_____

Action 2: Make a list of food items that you enjoy. See if there are items that you can eliminate or purchase at a cheaper price. Take some items from section 2 and develop your own recipes.

_____

_____

_____

_____

Action 3: Think of ways you can cut your entertainment budget?

_____

_____

_____

_____

Principle 2 Notes:

Principle 2 Thought Provoking Question:

How many items do I have that I thought I could not live without and I no longer use them or own them?

Reflection:

_____
_____
_____
_____
_____
_____
_____
_____
_____
_____
_____
_____
_____
_____
_____
_____
_____
_____
_____
_____
_____
_____
_____
_____
_____
_____
_____
_____

Principle 3: Payment Plans

Working with creditors is not always the easiest thing to do especially if your track record hasn't been the best. But, because of the current economic times creditors are more receptive to working with you and trying to develop payment plans to pay your debt off.

The first premise you must remember is it's not the creditors' fault you made poor financial decisions so don't get angry when the creditors call and want their money. Often times we run from creditors, lie to creditors, or thanks to caller id, simply don't pick up the phone. But that's the worst route you can take. It's better to be proactive rather than reactive especially if you are trying to eliminate your debt. Your demeanor can determine how the creditor interacts with you. If you are hostile, the creditor will be more hostile and at the end of the day, both of you will be nothing more than frustrated. So, let's walk through some ways of establishing manageable yet relevant payment plans that everyone can live with.

Tips for Payment Plans

The first thing you need to do is make a list of all your creditors and what you owe them. There's no way of getting out of debt without calculating what your debt is.

Without knowing this key information, you're hiking in the hills without a compass. You will find yourself passing the same marker multiple times or walking the same path for hours, only to end up in the same place, no where. The old adage 'he who fails to plan, plans to fail' certainly applies in this case.

Below is a worksheet to record your debt.

Current Bills	Payoff Amount

The second step is to itemize your list. Categorize your bills into several piles: largest to smallest payoff, highest to lowest percentage, and longest to shortest time for payoff. The objective of this step is to understand the debt you are faced with. As they say, 'a picture is worth a thousand words'. Analyze the 'picture' and determine what you can pay on each bill and how long it will take you to pay it off, if that amount is applied. If you can visualize the light at the end of the tunnel, then you will be more likely to stick to the plan. There are several money management tools you can invest in to help with this process. You can also use a simple spreadsheet to help you visualize your freedom but Quicken was an eye-opener for me. Being able to see when I could scream "I'm free" helped me commit to the plan.

Now, start making phone calls and have your information readily available in

front of you. Explain to the creditors that you would like to pay your debt off, but you only have a certain amount to apply to the bill each month. Some of the creditors will stop interest payments, lower your interest rate or even setup automatic payments to get you to the end of your goal. Don't get discouraged if some creditors don't agree to work with you; persistence is the key. If you continue to make payments regularly and on time, it can open a door or window a couple months later.

Other payment plans to consider are your everyday bills: utility, home and/or car insurance, etc. There are many utility companies that offer average payment plans. You can spread the cost of your utilities over several months so during peak seasons your bill will not skyrocket and cause your budget to crash. Also consider combining insurances like home and car to take advantage of discounts. Evaluate the type of coverage you have and if it's really necessary. Every little amount saved can be applied to reducing your debt.

Principle 3 Work Lessons:

Action 1: Identify the date you will have recorded all your bills, itemized them, and called creditors?

Bills listed: _____

Bills itemized: _____

Creditors Contacted By: _____

Action 2: Identify the other bills that could possibly be consolidated?

_____

_____

_____

_____

Action 3: Research your state's programs and identify other bills that you could establish payment plans.

_____

_____

_____

_____

Principle 3 Notes:

_____

_____

_____

_____

_____

_____

_____

_____

_____

_____

_____

If someone owed me money, would I prefer them to pay me back a little at a time, not at all, or a lump sum years from now?

Reflection:

Principle 4: Save Something

Most of us had the proverbial piggy bank when we were little and our parents taught us to save our coins for a rainy day. But somewhere along the way, this concept was lost for many of us for many different reasons. The reason most commonly used is '*I can't afford to save*'. And when you are under a pile of debt it is very hard to see how you can save any money at all. But saving is a concept that is vital to your financial stability. Without a rainy day fund, any little hiccup will throw a curve in your road to financial freedom. It's not that you will never get to the end of the road; but something will come along and start a construction project to extend your road, delaying completion. It's those discouraging, faith-shaking road extensions that will become the stepping stones to help you make it from under the heavy load of debt. So, it's not that you can't afford to save, you can't afford not to.

Here are some ways that you can save during tough situations: standard savings account, employee stock purchase programs, employee 401k plans, and remembering principle #2: learn to live on less so you can live on more.

Standard Saving Account

If you do nothing else, at least have a standard savings account. If you can only place $10 a paycheck into the account, do it. Without touching the account, after awhile you will find that you have saved more than you thought possible. Many standard savings accounts will yield at least 2% interest.

Employee Stock Purchase Programs

Many companies have employee stock purchase programs. This is a good way to invest back into your company while saving money at the same time. You can elect to have a certain amount of money applied each pay check to purchase your company's stock. If you allow your stock to build up, it can turn into a good rainy day fund for last minute emergencies. This is a savings option that you could get access to and cash in immediately, if you had to.

401k Plans

This option is more for future retirement savings planning. However, if you are in a real bind, you can take out a loan against your fund. 401k plans or equivalent programs are a great savings option because many companies match whatever you contribute. You can't beat saving money and having your employer match your efforts. You can quickly build up a nest egg and for emergency situations, access the account with relative ease.

Lastly, another way to save money is to remember principle #2: live on less to live on more. If you can master that principle, you will find countless ways to save more, not just to reduce debt, but also to augment your savings. Often times we spend unnecessarily; whether it's being satisfied with what you have in your closet rather than purchasing that new outfit, brown bagging-it or cooking dinner rather than eating out. I am not suggesting that there's anything wrong with doing these things. Nonetheless, if you are in debt and really want to get out, will these things help you accomplish your goal? Some things are lawful, but not expedient. In other words, it may not hurt you and be detrimental, but it's surely not helping you. We have to be honest with ourselves and know our limits. If we were completely truthful, we would make better decisions that will lead us to be financially stable and better money managers.

Saving money has to become a part of your daily routine. You have to stop using excuses not to save and come up with reasons why you can. Let's come up with several ways you can begin saving today; I'll even start your list for you:

Ways to Save	How much will I save a week
1.Brown Bag Lunch	
2.	
3.	
4.	
5.	

Principle 4 Work Lessons:

Question 1: Does your company have an employee stock purchase program? _____ Are you currently participating in it? _____ If not, when will you start? _____

Question 2: Does your company have a 401k plan or equivalent program? _____ Are you currently participating in it? _____ If not, when will you start? _____

Action 1: List reasons why you can't afford not to save?

_____

_____

_____

_____

Challenge 1: Starting today, each time you receive change, place the change in your money collection jar. At the end of the month, count how much you were able to save.

Principle 4 Notes:

_____

_____

_____

_____

_____

_____

_____

_____

_____

_____

_____

_____

Principle 4 Thought Provoking Question:

If I had saved a penny a day starting at the age of 5, how much money would I have saved by now?

Reflection:

Principle 5: Turn Your Talent into Extra Income

Do you have a special gift or talent? Or can you think of anything that you love to do that others get paid for? Well, why haven't you turned your gift into cash? The more money you have to apply to your debt, the quicker you can pay it off. Being able to generate money outside of your normal 9 to 5 job can get you on the speedy recovery you so desire.

There are many things you can do to generate extra money. For instance:

Garage sales are a great way to not only clean out your clutter, but to generate some extra income. During these tough economic times, many people are looking for bargains and garage sales are a great way to pick up items you need but can't afford to pay full price for. If you need extra income, this is a perfect no hassle way to get it. Garage sales don't take a lot of planning, time, or marketing to pull off. All you have to do is organize your items, determine your prices, and put up a few neighborhood signs and jackpot! You will be surprised at how much you can make in one weekend on a simple garage sale.

Auction Sites

If you like to sell stuff, online auction sites are the perfect way to get rid of things as well. You will be surprised at what people will buy. To you it may be old junk, but to someone else it's classic. People sell electronics, memorabilia, clothes, you name it. You can literally set-up your own store online and watch the dollars roll-in. What better way to drill down your debt?

Mystery Shoppers

If you like to shop or visit restaurants, this is the perfect side gig for you. You can become a mystery shopper. Many retailers will pay good money for you to visit their establishments and rate their services, products and/or customer service. Make sure you sign up with a reputable mystery shopping company. It just takes a little research, but its well worth it. If you have to go to an establishment anyway to shop or dine out, why not get paid for it?

These are just some examples of ways you can make extra income. But if you have a select gift or talent, turn that talent into a side business. Remember, the goal is to get out of debt. And once you are out of debt, you might find that you enjoyed your business venture so much that you would like to do it full time. Take a moment to list some of your gifts and talents. Here are some ideas to spark your imagination:

Photography

Graphic Design

Pet Sitter

Wedding/Event Planner

Web Site Designer

Freelance Writer

Lawn Care

Housekeeper

I am good at:
1.
2.
3.
4.
5.
6.
7.
8.
9.
10.

Principle 5 Work Lessons:

Action 1: Take your list from above and come up with ways to make extra income based on the list?

_____

_____

_____

Question 1: If you could make extra income, list the bills you could pay off as a result:

_____

_____

_____

_____

Action 2: Identify a date you will put your plan into action?

_____

Action 3: Identify items in your house that you could sell via online auctions or garage sales?

_____

_____

_____

_____

Action 4: Set a date to sell your items.

_____

Principle 5 Notes:

_____

_____

_____

_____

_____

_____

_____

_____

_____

_____

_____

_____

_____

Principle 5 Thought Provoking Question:

Could I be sitting on the answer to my problem?

Reflection:

Principle 6: Go Green

GO GREEN

Going Green is the buzz word of today. I am a firm believer that we all must do our part in this world, whether it's lending a helping hand to someone in need or saving the world. However, going green will not only help our planet, it will help your pocket. There are some simple tricks I learned that can help you save money and make you feel good about doing your part at the same time:

1. Unplug electronics when not in use: This helps our planet use less energy, but it also keeps your electric bill down.

2. Set your thermostat a few degrees lower in the winter and a few degrees higher in the summer.

3. Wash clothes in cold water when you can and use a drying rack when possible.

4. Take shorter showers.

I know many of us don't consider these small things for putting money back in our pockets, but just think about how much these tiny adjustments add up over time.

There are also funding opportunities via the federal government for green home improvements. Check out: http://www.epa.gov/greenbuilding/tools/funding.htm. Going green can be a stimulus for our economy as well as your home.

Principle 6 Work Lessons:

Challenge: Find ways you can go green and save money at the same time.

_____

_____

_____

_____

_____

_____

_____

_____

_____

_____

_____

_____

Principle 6 Thought Provoking Question:

What would happen if each person committed to five green initiatives?

Reflection:

_____
_____
_____
_____
_____
_____
_____
_____
_____
_____
_____
_____
_____
_____
_____
_____
_____
_____
_____
_____
_____
_____
_____
_____
_____
_____
_____
_____
_____
_____
_____
_____

Principle 7: Don't forget Principles 1-6

Once you have achieved your goal of financial freedom, don't make the mistake of forgetting everything you learned to get you there. I will testify that I made this very mistake. I eliminated most of my debt in order to purchase my home. Once I signed the closing documents, instead of growing in my house I did everything in the first couple months and wound up right back in debt. Bad mistake and bad decision making. I have definitely learned my lesson this time.

So, once you reach the mountaintop, don't forget the climb that got your there.

Otherwise, you might find yourself tumbling down the side of the mountain only to have to climb again. Let's summarize all of the principles that are key to getting you out of debt:

Principle 1: The Law of Sowing and Reaping- This principle is your foundation. You must understand there is a fundamental law at work. What you sow is what you'll produce. If you sow good decisions about money, you will reap the benefits of what you have sown. Bad debt is nothing more than the result of bad financial decisions. Those financial decisions could have stemmed from a lack of understanding, the inability to wait, or a host of other things. Needless to say, it's cause and effect.

Principle 2: Learn to Live on Less to Live on More- This principle will help you maintain your sanity while trying to get out of debt. How you react during your time of lack will determine just how quickly you can get out. Learning how to enjoy a peanut butter and jelly sandwich as if it was steak is a true testament of your will power and character. If you can learn to be satisfied with little, just imagine how you will feel when there is no longer lack in your life.

Principle 3: Payment Plans- This principle can help you visualize just how long your journey may last. If you are proactive in working with your creditors, your journey may not be as long as originally projected.

Principle 4: Save Something- This principle will allow you to enjoy your freedom even more and keep you from being distracted by minor setbacks in your progress. If you learn this basic principle, your financial freedom will only taste sweeter.

Principle 5: Turn Your Talent into Extra Income- This principle will give you a boost and allow you to pay bills off quicker. You might just find that you can turn this side gig into a permanent one.

Principle 6: Go Green- This principle will allow you to save money and apply it elsewhere, while you help our planet. Each one of us has a responsibility to help make this world a better place.

Principle 7: Don't Forget Principles 1-6- Once you reach the mountaintop be diligent so you won't tumble back down.

Principle 7 Work Lessons:

Action 1: Summarize how you plan to apply these principles to your life.

_____

_____

_____

_____

Question 1: When do you expect to be debt free?

Proclamation: I expect to be debt free by _____ and I am starting my journey today!

Principle 7 Notes:

_____

_____

_____

_____

_____

_____

_____

_____

_____

_____

_____

Principle 7 Thought Provoking Question:

How important is being debt free to me?

Reflection:

Roadblocks

During your journey to financial freedom, there are several roadblocks. Roadblocks cause detours that may delay your financial stability or get you completely off track. These roadblocks can be avoided but it's up to you to let them know that they are not welcome. You can't allow them to take up residence. So, let's explore some of these roadblocks and ensure you escape them and have smooth passage.

Discouragement

Discouragement is the elephant of roadblocks. If you allow this roadblock to settle in, you will never reach the end of your goal. It can come in many forms: bad influences, focusing on the glass half empty, and/or sheer fatigue from your journey.

Oftentimes, bad influences feel good at first: trying to impress someone with that new pair of shoes or new outfit when your account is already low; friends influencing you to have a night on the town when you know you can't afford it; being encouraged to take money from your bills to purchase an item because you work hard and you think you deserve it. Yes, the new pair of shoes/outfit will look good and you may get compliments from a special interest, but after that two minute ego boost, the attention wears off. The night out on the town may wash your worries away, but only for that night; and the emotional attachment that special purchase offers will last for only a day. In the end, you will go home, review your budget, and then kick yourself. Then discouragement knocks on your door with an overnight bag because you will feel like you will never get out of this hole and live the life you so desire. But you have to be willing to have self control and not allow these things to have power over you. When you find yourself in these situations, just remember you rule them and not the other way around.

Glass half empty

Having the mindset that the glass is half empty instead of half full can be detrimental to your progress. If you continue to look at what's not right, you will only prevent yourself from seeing your bright future. The phrase *'can't see the forest for the trees'* certainly applies in this case. If

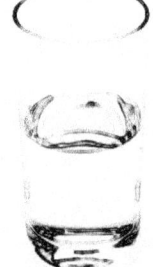

you continue to focus on [trees] what you can't do or what others have that you don't, you will never see the [forest] big picture. It's easy to allow this mentality to creep in, but once you open the door for this train of thought, discouragement will easily slither in along with it. I encourage you to look around and count your blessings. When we think we're bad off, if we truly consider it, there's someone else who really is worse off.

Sheer Fatigue

Exhaustion often causes our physical strength to diminish. But you have to recall *Rocky* in these times. Weariness is certainly a natural and understandable  condition. When you have exerted energy, it's only natural to want to rest. The only problem is this journey requires consistency and perseverance. So, in your times of weakness, dig deep down within yourself and pull from your adrenaline source. It's also important to have coaches in your corner to continue to push you and encourage you to keep fighting. *Rocky* never found his second wind until he was knocked down a couple times and his coaches and loved ones cheered, persuaded, and reinforced him. Fatigue will come, but if you have a good support team, you will quickly get a fresh wind and find yourself energized to keep going.

The key to avoiding this roadblock: learn to rule your surroundings, have a glass half full mentality, and surround yourself with others that lend strength instead of those that rob it. If you can do these things, **when** discouragement decides to visit, it will not stay long and you will have survived a roadblock.

Junk Mail

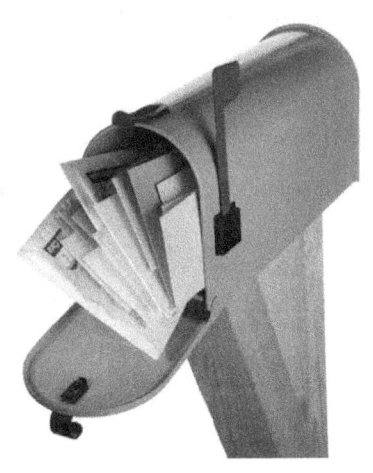

How many times have you opened the mailbox and found the credit card and loan offers just at the point when you needed a financial boost? And all of them say 'it's easy as 1-2-3', which makes you say to yourself, 'this is the answer'! The only problem is predatory lending is very real and,

well...predatory. They are not really concerned about helping you, only their bottom line. Usually the interest rates are sky high and by the time you pay this bill off, you would have paid for it several times over. Junk mail is a roadblock and ambushes you just when you're making headway with your financial goals. It often masks itself as the answer, but in the long run it only hinders you.

So, the cure to this roadblock: a shredder! A shredder is a worthwhile investment; one you will want to make to help alleviate this problem. As you receive these offers in the mail, take them directly to the shredder. You will find strength in turning this junk into little pieces of paper and you can also apply Principle 6 by recycling the paper!

Scams

In this technological age, scams are rampant with unsuspecting people who are looking for an easy way to the journey to financial freedom. From emails claiming you have won money from continents you have never visited to pyramid schemes or investment rip-offs, they come in many different forms. However, you have to be able to weed through the illusion these scams present. One you have to be aware of is offers to become debt-free. Many companies claim they can help to reduce or get you out of debt by working with your creditors for a fee. This is the first sign that something isn't kosher because with a little hard work and research, you can do yourself what they are offering to do for a price. You don't need a company to clean up your credit; you have every right to check your credit report and file claims if discrepancies appear. Be careful of companies offering you an oasis in a desert.

Another scam to be watchful of is get rich quick promises. Many pyramid plans and investment opportunities claim high returns with little buy-in. Generally, the high returns only apply to the mastermind. The phrase 'if it's too good to be true then it probably is' comes to mind. Getting rich, at whatever level, often requires hard work and nothing in this life is free. There's always a cost associated even if it's not apparent. Avoid this roadblock by simply testing the source: question the intent, contact the better business bureau, research the company, ask others, and use good old common sense. Remember, if it were that easy everyone would probably do it!

These are just some of the roadblocks that come to mind and I have encountered in some way or another. Some I succumbed to and learned a valuable lesson and others I avoided like the plague. If you want to continue on your road to financial freedom without interruption, put up a Do Not Enter sign for these roadblocks.

Conclusion

I learned these seven principles over the last year. Some I learned in past years, but it wasn't until this year that all of them jelled to become a reality for me. A major part of getting out of debt is a mind and attitude change. You have to make up in your mind that nothing will stand in your way of financial freedom. You have to have an attitude change to realize that others around you can't affect your finances; only you can. You have to stop waiting for the money tree to grow in your yard to solve your problems. Your financial stability is tied to the decisions you make and you can start by making better ones today. It took time for you to create the hole you are in so don't expect to dig your way out overnight. But, with creativity, persistence, and a made up mind it won't take as long as you think.

I am still learning each and every day, but I am determined to make it to the end of my journey. I am excited about sharing with you what I learned and hope that my experiences will help you get to a place of fulfillment and joy in your finances. I hope that you will join me on the road to financial freedom and I hope to see you at the finish line.

FINANCIAL FREEDOM

Appendix

Tips and Tricks

Tip: Order your free credit reports from the three credit agencies annually. The free credit report link is www.annualcreditreport.com.

Tip: Re-evaluate your tax deductions to ensure you aren't paying too much in taxes. You can use the money up-front to pay your bills down rather than receiving a refund each year.

Tip: Don't get caught up in seasonal/holiday hype! Only purchase what you can afford. If you can't afford anything, be creative. Make homemade gifts or simply show your love in other ways.

Trick: Save money by using items multiple ways and times.

Tip: Learn how to perform services yourself you would normally pay for: nails, hair, etc.

Tip: Purchase items with cash or debit card only, not on credit.

Tip: Sign-up for your favorite restaurant's mailing list to receive coupons and free offers if you want to eat out now and then.

Trick: Conserve gas by planning and restricting errands to the same area of town.

Tip: Consider planting a small garden of your favorite vegetables to save money.

Tip: Learn a new skill and do some home repairs yourself.

Tip: Get reputable referrals for local car repairmen instead of going to the dealership's service center.

Tip: Setup automatic payments for your bills once you have established a payment plan with your creditor(s).

Workbook References

Budget Planner

First: Track all your expenses for four weeks. Write down everything you purchase, even vending machine items.

	Sun	Mon	Tues	Wed	Thurs	Fri	Sat
Week 1							
Week 2							
Week 3							
Week 4							

Second: Eliminate items that you feel you can do without (remember Principle 2).

Eliminated Expense	Average Amount Spent
Total Savings:	

Tip: Divert this total to your savings account

Third: Write down your monthly income

Sheet 1: Income Sheet

Salary	
Extra Income	
Other Sources	
Total Income:	

Fourth: Write down your monthly expenses

Sheet 2: Expense Sheet

Expenses	Average Amount
Tithes/Offering (remember Principle 1)	
Rent/Mortgage	
Insurance (car, home, medical, life, etc)	
Utilities (light, gas, water, trash, sewer, etc)	
Car (note/lease, oil change/maintenance, gas, tags)	
Groceries	
Total Expenses	

Fifth: Calculate your monthly surplus/deficit

Sheet 3: Totals

Total Income (Sheet 1)	
Total Expenses (Sheet 2)	
Profit/Loss	

Sixth: Create a twelve month calendar and enter your totals for each month. Add/subtract your profit or loss to/from the next month and calculate your new totals.

Online Budget Resources:

If you have access to the internet, you can use the following free online resources to create your monthly budget.

Free Quicken Online: http://quicken.intuit.com/personal-finance-software/free-online-money-management.jsp

Microsoft Excel Templates: http://office.microsoft.com/en-us/templates/CT101172321033.aspx

Meal Planner

Low Cost Meal Sample

	Sun	Mon	Tues	Wed	Thurs	Fri	Sat
Breakfast	Whole Grain Toast, Eggs	Oatmeal	Fruit Smoothie	Fruit and Whole Grain Toast	Omelet	Oatmeal	Omelet
Lunch		Peanut Butter/Jelly Sandwich, Apple	Salad	Turkey Sandwich on Whole Grain	Tuna Fish Sandwich on Whole Grain		
Dinner	Cabbage, Grilled Chicken	Leftovers	Brandie's Mix over Brown Rice	Leftovers	Whole Grain Pasta with Vegetable Primavera	Fried Rice with Brown Rice	Leftovers
Dessert	Ice cream		Pineapple		Apples and Caramel		

Ingredients for these meals can normally stretch for two weeks (approximate cost $60).

Create Your Own

	Sun	Mon	Tues	Wed	Thurs	Fri	Sat
Breakfast							
Lunch							
Dinner							
Dessert							

Payment Plan Register

Creditor	Agreed to Payment Plan (Y/N)	Follow-up Date

Online Tax Resources

IRS Withholding Calculator:
http://www.irs.gov/individuals/page/0,,id=14806,00.html

IRS:
http://www.efile.com/tax-service/tax-calculator/2009-tax-calculator/

Turbo Tax:
http://www.express-tax-refund.com/

Online Savings Resources

U.S. Department of Labor Employee Benefits Security Administration (EBSA):

Your Savings Fitness: http://www.dol.gov/ebsa/PDF/savingsfitness.pdf

Online Credit Repair Resources

Federal Trade Commission: Credit Repair How to Help Yourself

http://www.ftc.gov/bcp/edu/pubs/consumer/credit/cre13.pdf

Online Calculator Resources

Roll Down Debt Calculator:

http://calculators.interest.com/content/calculators/new/roll-downdebt.asp

Savings Calculator:

http://calculators.interest.com/content/calculators/savingscalc.asp

401k Calculator:

http://www.bloomberg.com/invest/calculators/401k.html

Payroll Deductions Calculator:

http://www.bloomberg.com/invest/calculators/payroll.html

Debt Consolidation Calculator:

http://www.bloomberg.com/invest/calculators/consolidate.html

Know Your Rights

Dealing with Debt Collectors

The Fair Debt Collection Practices Act (FDCPA) applies to personal, family, and household debts. This includes money you owe for the purchase of a car, for medical care, or for charge accounts. The FDCPA prohibits debt collectors from engaging in unfair, deceptive, or abusive practices while collecting these debts. Under the Fair Debt Collection Practices Act:

- Debt collectors may contact you only between 8 a.m. and 9 p.m.

- Debt collectors may not contact you at work if they know your employer disapproves.

- Debt collectors may not harass, oppress, or abuse you.

- Debt collectors may not lie when collecting debts, such as falsely implying that you have committed a crime.

- Debt collectors must identify themselves to you on the phone.

- Debt collectors must stop contacting you if you ask them to do so in writing.

Information source: Federal Trade Commission March 2005 issue author – FTC
http://www.ftc.gov/bcp/edu/pubs/consumer/credit/cre01.shtm

Debt Collection FAQs: A Guide for Consumers

http://www.ftc.gov/bcp/edu/pubs/consumer/credit/cre18.shtm

Consumer Opt-Out: You have the right to decide whether your information is shared

http://www.ftc.gov/privacy/protect.shtm

Proclamation

Begin to verbalize what you want to experience. Your words can influence your surroundings. The more you speak it, the more it becomes a part of you.

Read Out Loud

I am on the road to becoming debt free. I will commit to the process and experience. I am in this current situation because of decisions I have made or because I have allowed others to affect my finances. I will no longer blame others for my problems. Today, I proclaim that I will no longer live outside of my means. I will defer gratification today to experience financial freedom tomorrow. Each day will take renewing my commitment to the process, but I am willing to take that step. Before I make decisions that can affect my finances, I will ask myself, how will this purchase or decision affect my ability to get out of debt? I will no longer make emotionally charged, peer persuaded, self-indulged purchases. I will leave my past in the past and I will take back control over my finances. Today, I step closer to financial freedom. I proclaim I will live a debt free life!

End Note

I would like to applaud you for taking steps to gaining your financial freedom. It's easier to complain about our current situations, but it takes courage to admit and take responsibility for the financial situation we have placed ourselves in. Getting your finances in control can unlock a world of possibilities that seemed closed to you before. Being a good steward over what passes through your hands will only prepare you to manage much more.

No matter what your financial goals may be, the key to reaching your goal is to remain honest with yourself. Don't allow others to dictate your financial stability. Always remember, their perception of you is not your reality. You can't afford to allow peer pressure, gluttony, or a sheer lack of self control hinder you from living a debt free life.

The concept of Moolah is understood in every language: money (English), dinero (Spanish), denaro (Italian), dinheiro (Portuguese), paper/cheese/benjamins (slang), and the list goes on and on. No matter what language you speak, Moolah is universal. The objective of the 7 Principles of Getting Out of Debt is to keep and save more Moolah (money) for yourself.

Live a prosperous and debt free life!

If you would like to share your success stories/comments as a result of this book and/or encouragement, please send an email to moolah_principles@hotmail.com.

Notes:

_____
_____
_____
_____
_____
_____
_____
_____
_____
_____
_____
_____
_____
_____
_____
_____
_____
_____
_____
_____
_____
_____
_____
_____

Notes:

Notes:

Notes:

_____

_____

_____

_____

_____

_____

_____

_____

_____

_____

_____

_____

_____

_____

_____

_____

_____

_____

_____

_____

_____

_____

_____

Notes:

_____
_____
_____
_____
_____
_____
_____
_____
_____
_____
_____
_____
_____
_____
_____
_____
_____
_____
_____
_____
_____
_____
_____
_____
_____
_____

Notes:

Notes: